It's a Dog's Life

A journal for dogs and their people who like to walk, explore, and have adventures.

By
Pam Robertson

This book is dedicated
to my sister, Lynda.

All Rights Reserved. No part of this book may be used or reproduced in any manner whatsoever without written permission from the author, except in the case of brief quotations embodied in critical articles or reviews.

The author and publisher (that's Pam in case you are wondering) have made every effort to ensure that the information in this book was correct at press time and do not assume any liability to any party due to this book coming from the author's own personal experience and opinion. This information is considered a tad educational and totally recreational.

WARNING: Journal writing in such a stonktastic book as this has been known to lead to scrap booking. If you paste an image of you and your companions on the front cover to make it look even cooler than it already does, you have scrap booked. This kind of behaviour is strongly encouraged as you make the journal a conversation piece, and something you are proud to own.

Also, I'd appreciate it if you would resist pinching the idea for this whizzy little book. I've already spent weeks on it and I'm absolutely certain that if you put your mind to it, you can come up with something that's brilliant and all yours, too. If you're having trouble coming up with something, then by all means go for a nice long walk and think it over. You're bound to come up with something, just as I did. You can call me if you'd like some help.

Pam Robertson | Call 780-232-0083
Facebook BeBoldBeBraveBeBrilliant Twitter @PamRobertson
IG @PamDRobertson www.ladybirdfiles.com

(c) Pam Robertson 2016
Cover photo by Pam Robertson
Published by Pam Robertson Consulting Inc.

ISBN 978-0-9918569-6-1

Every Dog Has its Day!

I created this journal so that every time you take your dog out on a walk or adventure, you can have some fun describing your outing. One element of the fun is that I am encouraging you to write everything from the dog's point of view.

You can turn this journal into a full on scrapbook if you'd like, by adding little tidbits like a printed photo, a map of where you went (maps that show the dog's tracks are usually priceless), how much fun your four legged friend had, and more. The options are endless!

This book can be a great way to look back and figure out things like dog behaviour, where the best tasting sticks are, and of course it also helps you to keep track of problems. Not that our dogs have many problems, but sometimes there is a stick that leads to an upset stomach, a poorly behaved dog you meet, or a park without fences along a busy road.

You can also keep track of treats, bodily functions, and anything your vet might like to know at an upcoming visit by keeping your entries up to date.

I hope you and your four legged friends have many wonderful adventures together, and lots to write about!

Love,
Pam

The Essentials

This page is handy for recording important numbers and information that your people may need to refer to now and again. This information is especially helpful if you go on an adventure on your own and they are having trouble finding you.

Your name _____
Your person's name _____
Microchip number _____
Breed(s) _____
Colour(s) _____
Height/Weight _____
Medications _____
Allergies _____
Health conditions _____

Look! Space to paste a picture or draw one!

Date: _____

We went to: _____

We saw: _____

We met: _____

I had _____ treats during this adventure!

I pooped _____ time(s) while I was out!

Notes for pawsterity about today:

🐾 _____
_____
_____
_____
_____
_____

Use this space for drawings, pasting pictures, paw prints, or whatever you feel like saving in your journal.

Date: _____

We went to: _____

We saw: _____

We met: _____

I had _____ treats during this adventure!

I pooped _____ time(s) while I was out!

Notes for pawsterity about today:

🐾 _____
_____
_____
_____
_____
_____

Use this space for drawings, pasting pictures, paw prints, or whatever you feel like saving in your journal.

Date: _____

We went to: _____

We saw: _____

We met: _____

I had _____ treats during this adventure!

I pooped _____ time(s) while I was out!

Notes for pawsterity about today:

🐾 _____
_____
_____
_____
_____
_____

Use this space for drawings, pasting pictures, paw prints, or whatever you feel like saving in your journal.

Date: _____

We went to: _____

We saw: _____

We met: _____

I had _____ treats during this adventure!

I pooped _____ time(s) while I was out!

Notes for pawsterity about today:

🐾 _____
_____
_____
_____
_____
_____

Use this space for drawings, pasting pictures, paw prints, or whatever you feel like saving in your journal.

Date: _____

We went to: _____

We saw: _____

We met: _____

I had _____ treats during this adventure!

I pooped _____ time(s) while I was out!

Notes for pawsterity about today:

🐾 _____
_____
_____
_____
_____
_____

Use this space for drawings, pasting pictures, paw prints, or whatever you feel like saving in your journal.

Date: _____

We went to: _____

We saw: _____

We met: _____

I had _____ treats during this adventure!

I pooped _____ time(s) while I was out!

Notes for pawsterity about today:

🐾 _____
_____
_____
_____
_____
_____

Use this space for drawings, pasting pictures, paw prints, or whatever you feel like saving in your journal.

Date: _____

We went to: _____

We saw: _____

We met: _____

I had _____ treats during this adventure!

I pooped _____ time(s) while I was out!

Notes for pawsterity about today:

🐾 _____
_____
_____
_____
_____
_____

Use this space for drawings, pasting pictures, paw prints, or whatever you feel like saving in your journal.

Date: _____

We went to: _____

We saw: _____

We met: _____

I had _____ treats during this adventure!

I pooped _____ time(s) while I was out!

Notes for pawsterity about today:

🐾 _____
_____
_____
_____
_____
_____

Use this space for drawings, pasting pictures, paw prints, or whatever you feel like saving in your journal.

Date: _____

We went to: _____

We saw: _____

We met: _____

I had _____ treats during this adventure!

I pooped _____ time(s) while I was out!

Notes for pawsterity about today:

🐾 _____
_____
_____
_____
_____

Use this space for drawings, pasting pictures, paw prints, or whatever you feel like saving in your journal.

Date: _____

We went to: _____

We saw: _____

We met: _____

I had _____ treats during this adventure!

I pooped _____ time(s) while I was out!

Notes for pawsterity about today:

🐾 _____
_____
_____
_____
_____
_____

Use this space for drawings, pasting pictures, paw prints, or whatever you feel like saving in your journal.

Date: _____

We went to: _____

We saw: _____

We met: _____

I had _____ treats during this adventure!

I pooped _____ time(s) while I was out!

Notes for pawsterity about today:

🐾 _____
_____
_____
_____
_____
_____

Use this space for drawings, pasting pictures, paw prints, or whatever you feel like saving in your journal.

Date: _____

We went to: _____

We saw: _____

We met: _____

I had _____ treats during this adventure!

I pooped _____ time(s) while I was out!

Notes for pawsterity about today:

🐾 _____
_____
_____
_____
_____
_____

Use this space for drawings, pasting pictures, paw prints, or whatever you feel like saving in your journal.

Date: _____

We went to: _____

We saw: _____

We met: _____

I had _____ treats during this adventure!

I pooped _____ time(s) while I was out!

Notes for pawsterity about today:

🐾 _____
_____
_____
_____
_____
_____

Use this space for drawings, pasting pictures, paw prints, or whatever you feel like saving in your journal.

Date: _____

We went to: _____

We saw: _____

We met: _____

I had _____ treats during this adventure!

I pooped _____ time(s) while I was out!

Notes for pawsterity about today:

🐾 _____
_____
_____
_____
_____
_____

Use this space for drawings, pasting pictures, paw prints, or whatever you feel like saving in your journal.

Date: _____

We went to: _____

We saw: _____

We met: _____

I had _____ treats during this adventure!

I pooped _____ time(s) while I was out!

Notes for pawsterity about today:

🐾 _____
_____
_____
_____
_____
_____

Use this space for drawings, pasting pictures, paw prints, or whatever you feel like saving in your journal.

Date: _____

We went to: _____

We saw: _____

We met: _____

I had _____ treats during this adventure!

I pooped _____ time(s) while I was out!

Notes for pawsterity about today:

🐾 _____
_____
_____
_____
_____
_____

Use this space for drawings, pasting pictures, paw prints, or whatever you feel like saving in your journal.

Date: _____

We went to: _____

We saw: _____

We met: _____

I had _____ treats during this adventure!

I pooped _____ time(s) while I was out!

Notes for pawsterity about today:

🐾 _____
_____
_____
_____
_____
_____

Use this space for drawings, pasting pictures, paw prints, or whatever you feel like saving in your journal.

Date: _____

We went to: _____

We saw: _____

We met: _____

I had _____ treats during this adventure!

I pooped _____ time(s) while I was out!

Notes for pawsterity about today:

🐾 _____
_____
_____
_____
_____
_____

Use this space for drawings, pasting pictures, paw prints, or whatever you feel like saving in your journal.

Date: _____

We went to: _____

We saw: _____

We met: _____

I had _____ treats during this adventure!

I pooped _____ time(s) while I was out!

Notes for pawsterity about today:

🐾 _____
_____
_____
_____
_____
_____

Use this space for drawings, pasting pictures, paw prints, or whatever you feel like saving in your journal.

Date: _____

We went to: _____

We saw: _____

We met: _____

I had _____ treats during this adventure!

I pooped _____ time(s) while I was out!

Notes for pawsterity about today:

🐾 _____
_____
_____
_____
_____
_____

Use this space for drawings, pasting pictures, paw prints, or whatever you feel like saving in your journal.

Date: _____

We went to: _____

We saw: _____

We met: _____

I had _____ treats during this adventure!

I pooped _____ time(s) while I was out!

Notes for pawsterity about today:

🐾 _____
_____
_____
_____
_____
_____

Use this space for drawings, pasting pictures, paw prints, or whatever you feel like saving in your journal.

Date: _____

We went to: _____

We saw: _____

We met: _____

I had _____ treats during this adventure!

I pooped _____ time(s) while I was out!

Notes for pawsterity about today:

🐾 _____
_____
_____
_____
_____
_____
_____

Use this space for drawings, pasting pictures, paw prints, or whatever you feel like saving in your journal.

Date: _____

We went to: _____

We saw: _____

We met: _____

I had _____ treats during this adventure!

I pooped _____ time(s) while I was out!

Notes for pawsterity about today:

🐾 _____
_____
_____
_____
_____
_____

Use this space for drawings, pasting pictures, paw prints, or whatever you feel like saving in your journal.

Date: _____

We went to: _____

We saw: _____

We met: _____

I had _____ treats during this adventure!

I pooped _____ time(s) while I was out!

Notes for pawsterity about today:

🐾 _____
_____
_____
_____
_____
_____

Use this space for drawings, pasting pictures, paw prints, or whatever you feel like saving in your journal.

Date: _____

We went to: _____

We saw: _____

We met: _____

I had _____ treats during this adventure!

I pooped _____ time(s) while I was out!

Notes for pawsterity about today:

🐾 _____
_____
_____
_____
_____
_____

Use this space for drawings, pasting pictures, paw prints, or whatever you feel like saving in your journal.

Date: _____

We went to: _____

We saw: _____

We met: _____

I had _____ treats during this adventure!

I pooped _____ time(s) while I was out!

Notes for pawsterity about today:

🐾 _____
_____
_____
_____
_____
_____

Use this space for drawings, pasting pictures, paw prints, or whatever you feel like saving in your journal.

Date: _____

We went to: _____

We saw: _____

We met: _____

I had _____ treats during this adventure!

I pooped _____ time(s) while I was out!

Notes for pawsterity about today:

🐾 _____
_____
_____
_____
_____
_____

Use this space for drawings, pasting pictures, paw prints, or whatever you feel like saving in your journal.

Date: _____

We went to: _____

We saw: _____

We met: _____

I had _____ treats during this adventure!

I pooped _____ time(s) while I was out!

Notes for pawsterity about today:

🐾 _____
_____
_____
_____
_____
_____

Use this space for drawings, pasting pictures, paw prints, or whatever you feel like saving in your journal.

Date: _____

We went to: _____

We saw: _____

We met: _____

I had _____ treats during this adventure!

I pooped _____ time(s) while I was out!

Notes for pawsterity about today:

🐾 _____
_____
_____
_____
_____
_____

Use this space for drawings, pasting pictures, paw prints, or whatever you feel like saving in your journal.

Date: _____

We went to: _____

We saw: _____

We met: _____

I had _____ treats during this adventure!

I pooped _____ time(s) while I was out!

Notes for pawsterity about today:

🐾 _____
_____
_____
_____
_____
_____

Use this space for drawings, pasting pictures, paw prints, or whatever you feel like saving in your journal.

Date: _____

We went to: _____

We saw: _____

We met: _____

I had _____ treats during this adventure!

I pooped _____ time(s) while I was out!

Notes for pawsterity about today:

🐾 _____
_____
_____
_____
_____
_____

Use this space for drawings, pasting pictures, paw prints, or whatever you feel like saving in your journal.

Date: _____

We went to: _____

We saw: _____

We met: _____

I had _____ treats during this adventure!

I pooped _____ time(s) while I was out!

Notes for pawsterity about today:

🐾 _____
_____
_____
_____
_____
_____

Use this space for drawings, pasting pictures, paw prints, or whatever you feel like saving in your journal.

Date: _____

We went to: _____

We saw: _____

We met: _____

I had _____ treats during this adventure!

I pooped _____ time(s) while I was out!

Notes for pawsterity about today:

🐾 _____
_____
_____
_____
_____
_____

Use this space for drawings, pasting pictures, paw prints, or whatever you feel like saving in your journal.

Date: _____

We went to: _____

We saw: _____

We met: _____

I had _____ treats during this adventure!

I pooped _____ time(s) while I was out!

Notes for pawsterity about today:

🐾 _____
_____
_____
_____
_____
_____

Use this space for drawings, pasting pictures, paw prints, or whatever you feel like saving in your journal.

Date: _____

We went to: _____

We saw: _____

We met: _____

I had _____ treats during this adventure!

I pooped _____ time(s) while I was out!

Notes for pawsterity about today:

🐾 _____
_____
_____
_____
_____
_____

Use this space for drawings, pasting pictures, paw prints, or whatever you feel like saving in your journal.

Date: _____

We went to: _____

We saw: _____

We met: _____

I had _____ treats during this adventure!

I pooped _____ time(s) while I was out!

Notes for pawsterity about today:

🐾 _____
_____
_____
_____
_____
_____

Use this space for drawings, pasting pictures, paw prints, or whatever you feel like saving in your journal.

Date: _____

We went to: _____

We saw: _____

We met: _____

I had _____ treats during this adventure!

I pooped _____ time(s) while I was out!

Notes for pawsterity about today:

🐾 _____
_____
_____
_____
_____
_____

Use this space for drawings, pasting pictures, paw prints, or whatever you feel like saving in your journal.

Date: _____

We went to: _____

We saw: _____

We met: _____

I had _____ treats during this adventure!

I pooped _____ time(s) while I was out!

Notes for pawsterity about today:

🐾 _____
_____
_____
_____
_____
_____

Use this space for drawings, pasting pictures, paw prints, or whatever you feel like saving in your journal.

Date: _____

We went to: _____

We saw: _____

We met: _____

I had _____ treats during this adventure!

I pooped _____ time(s) while I was out!

Notes for pawsterity about today:

🐾 _____
_____
_____
_____
_____
_____

Use this space for drawings, pasting pictures, paw prints, or whatever you feel like saving in your journal.

Date: _____

We went to: _____

We saw: _____

We met: _____

I had _____ treats during this adventure!

I pooped _____ time(s) while I was out!

Notes for pawsterity about today:

🐾 _____
_____
_____
_____
_____
_____

Use this space for drawings, pasting pictures, paw prints, or whatever you feel like saving in your journal.

Date: _____

We went to: _____

We saw: _____

We met: _____

I had _____ treats during this adventure!

I pooped _____ time(s) while I was out!

Notes for pawsterity about today:

🐾 _____
_____
_____
_____
_____
_____

Use this space for drawings, pasting pictures, paw prints, or whatever you feel like saving in your journal.

Date: _____

We went to: _____

We saw: _____

We met: _____

I had _____ treats during this adventure!

I pooped _____ time(s) while I was out!

Notes for pawsterity about today:

🐾 _____
_____
_____
_____
_____
_____

Use this space for drawings, pasting pictures, paw prints, or whatever you feel like saving in your journal.

Date: _____
We went to: _____
We saw: _____
We met: _____
I had _____ treats during this adventure!
I pooped _____ time(s) while I was out!
Notes for pawsterity about today:

🐾 _____
_____
_____
_____
_____
_____

Use this space for drawings, pasting pictures, paw prints, or whatever you feel like saving in your journal.

Date: _____

We went to: _____

We saw: _____

We met: _____

I had _____ treats during this adventure!

I pooped _____ time(s) while I was out!

Notes for pawsterity about today:

🐾 _____
_____
_____
_____
_____
_____

Use this space for drawings, pasting pictures, paw prints, or whatever you feel like saving in your journal.

Date: _____

We went to: _____

We saw: _____

We met: _____

I had _____ treats during this adventure!

I pooped _____ time(s) while I was out!

Notes for pawsterity about today:

_____
_____
_____
_____
_____
_____

Use this space for drawings, pasting pictures, paw prints, or whatever you feel like saving in your journal.

Date: _____

We went to: _____

We saw: _____

We met: _____

I had _____ treats during this adventure!

I pooped _____ time(s) while I was out!

Notes for pawsterity about today:

🐾 _____
_____
_____
_____
_____
_____

Use this space for drawings, pasting pictures, paw prints, or whatever you feel like saving in your journal.

Date: _____

We went to: _____

We saw: _____

We met: _____

I had _____ treats during this adventure!

I pooped _____ time(s) while I was out!

Notes for pawsterity about today:

🐾 _____
_____
_____
_____
_____
_____

Use this space for drawings, pasting pictures, paw prints, or whatever you feel like saving in your journal.

Date: _____

We went to: _____

We saw: _____

We met: _____

I had _____ treats during this adventure!

I pooped _____ time(s) while I was out!

Notes for pawsterity about today:

🐾 _____
_____
_____
_____
_____
_____

Use this space for drawings, pasting pictures, paw prints, or whatever you feel like saving in your journal.

Date: _____

We went to: _____

We saw: _____

We met: _____

I had _____ treats during this adventure!

I pooped _____ time(s) while I was out!

Notes for pawsterity about today:

🐾 _____
_____
_____
_____
_____
_____

Use this space for drawings, pasting pictures, paw prints, or whatever you feel like saving in your journal.

Date: _____

We went to: _____

We saw: _____

We met: _____

I had _____ treats during this adventure!

I pooped _____ time(s) while I was out!

Notes for pawsterity about today:

🐾 _____
_____
_____
_____
_____
_____

Use this space for drawings, pasting pictures, paw prints, or whatever you feel like saving in your journal.

Date: _____

We went to: _____

We saw: _____

We met: _____

I had _____ treats during this adventure!

I pooped _____ time(s) while I was out!

Notes for pawsterity about today:

🐾 _____
_____
_____
_____
_____
_____

Use this space for drawings, pasting pictures, paw prints, or whatever you feel like saving in your journal.

Date: _____
We went to: _____
We saw: _____
We met: _____
I had _____ treats during this adventure!
I pooped _____ time(s) while I was out!
Notes for pawsterity about today:

🐾 _____
_____
_____
_____
_____
_____

Use this space for drawings, pasting pictures, paw prints, or whatever you feel like saving in your journal.

Date: _____

We went to: _____

We saw: _____

We met: _____

I had _____ treats during this adventure!

I pooped _____ time(s) while I was out!

Notes for pawsterity about today:

🐾 _____
_____
_____
_____
_____
_____

Use this space for drawings, pasting pictures, paw prints, or whatever you feel like saving in your journal.

Date: _____

We went to: _____

We saw: _____

We met: _____

I had _____ treats during this adventure!

I pooped _____ time(s) while I was out!

Notes for pawsterity about today:

🐾 _____
_____
_____
_____
_____
_____

Use this space for drawings, pasting pictures, paw prints, or whatever you feel like saving in your journal.

Date: _____

We went to: _____

We saw: _____

We met: _____

I had _____ treats during this adventure!

I pooped _____ time(s) while I was out!

Notes for pawsterity about today:

🐾 _____
_____
_____
_____
_____
_____

Use this space for drawings, pasting pictures, paw prints, or whatever you feel like saving in your journal.

Date: _____

We went to: _____

We saw: _____

We met: _____

I had _____ treats during this adventure!

I pooped _____ time(s) while I was out!

Notes for pawsterity about today:

🐾 _____
_____
_____
_____
_____
_____

Use this space for drawings, pasting pictures, paw prints, or whatever you feel like saving in your journal.

Date: _____

We went to: _____

We saw: _____

We met: _____

I had _____ treats during this adventure!

I pooped _____ time(s) while I was out!

Notes for pawsterity about today:

🐾 _____
_____
_____
_____
_____
_____

Use this space for drawings, pasting pictures, paw prints, or whatever you feel like saving in your journal.

Date: _____

We went to: _____

We saw: _____

We met: _____

I had _____ treats during this adventure!

I pooped _____ time(s) while I was out!

Notes for pawsterity about today:

🐾 _____
_____
_____
_____
_____
_____

Use this space for drawings, pasting pictures, paw prints, or whatever you feel like saving in your journal.

Date: _____

We went to: _____

We saw: _____

We met: _____

I had _____ treats during this adventure!

I pooped _____ time(s) while I was out!

Notes for pawsterity about today:

🐾 _____
_____
_____
_____
_____
_____

Use this space for drawings, pasting pictures, paw prints, or whatever you feel like saving in your journal.

Date: _____

We went to: _____

We saw: _____

We met: _____

I had _____ treats during this adventure!

I pooped _____ time(s) while I was out!

Notes for pawsterity about today:

🐾 _____
_____
_____
_____
_____
_____

Use this space for drawings, pasting pictures, paw prints, or whatever you feel like saving in your journal.

Date: _____

We went to: _____

We saw: _____

We met: _____

I had _____ treats during this adventure!

I pooped _____ time(s) while I was out!

Notes for pawsterity about today:

🐾 _____
_____
_____
_____
_____
_____

Use this space for drawings, pasting pictures, paw prints, or whatever you feel like saving in your journal.

Date: _____

We went to: _____

We saw: _____

We met: _____

I had _____ treats during this adventure!

I pooped _____ time(s) while I was out!

Notes for pawsterity about today:

🐾 _____
_____
_____
_____
_____
_____

Use this space for drawings, pasting pictures, paw prints, or whatever you feel like saving in your journal.

Date: _____

We went to: _____

We saw: _____

We met: _____

I had _____ treats during this adventure!

I pooped _____ time(s) while I was out!

Notes for pawsterity about today:

🐾 _____
_____
_____
_____
_____
_____

Use this space for drawings, pasting pictures, paw prints, or whatever you feel like saving in your journal.

Date: _____

We went to: _____

We saw: _____

We met: _____

I had _____ treats during this adventure!

I pooped _____ time(s) while I was out!

Notes for pawsterity about today:

🐾 _____
_____
_____
_____
_____
_____

Use this space for drawings, pasting pictures, paw prints, or whatever you feel like saving in your journal.

Date: _____

We went to: _____

We saw: _____

We met: _____

I had _____ treats during this adventure!

I pooped _____ time(s) while I was out!

Notes for pawsterity about today:

🐾 _____
_____
_____
_____
_____

Use this space for drawings, pasting pictures, paw prints, or whatever you feel like saving in your journal.

Date: _____

We went to: _____

We saw: _____

We met: _____

I had _____ treats during this adventure!

I pooped _____ time(s) while I was out!

Notes for pawsterity about today:

🐾 _____
_____
_____
_____
_____
_____

Use this space for drawings, pasting pictures, paw prints, or whatever you feel like saving in your journal.

Date: _____

We went to: _____

We saw: _____

We met: _____

I had _____ treats during this adventure!

I pooped _____ time(s) while I was out!

Notes for pawsterity about today:

🐾 _____
_____
_____
_____
_____
_____

Use this space for drawings, pasting pictures, paw prints, or whatever you feel like saving in your journal.

Date: _____

We went to: _____

We saw: _____

We met: _____

I had _____ treats during this adventure!

I pooped _____ time(s) while I was out!

Notes for pawsterity about today:

🐾 _____
_____
_____
_____
_____
_____

Use this space for drawings, pasting pictures, paw prints, or whatever you feel like saving in your journal.

Date: _____

We went to: _____

We saw: _____

We met: _____

I had _____ treats during this adventure!

I pooped _____ time(s) while I was out!

Notes for pawsterity about today:

🐾 _____
_____
_____
_____
_____
_____

Use this space for drawings, pasting pictures, paw prints, or whatever you feel like saving in your journal.

Date: _____

We went to: _____

We saw: _____

We met: _____

I had _____ treats during this adventure!

I pooped _____ time(s) while I was out!

Notes for pawsterity about today:

🐾 _____
_____
_____
_____
_____
_____

Use this space for drawings, pasting pictures, paw prints, or whatever you feel like saving in your journal.

Date: _____

We went to: _____

We saw: _____

We met: _____

I had _____ treats during this adventure!

I pooped _____ time(s) while I was out!

Notes for pawsterity about today:

🐾 _____
_____
_____
_____
_____
_____

Use this space for drawings, pasting pictures, paw prints, or whatever you feel like saving in your journal.

Date: _____

We went to: _____

We saw: _____

We met: _____

I had _____ treats during this adventure!

I pooped _____ time(s) while I was out!

Notes for pawsterity about today:

🐾 _____
   _____
   _____
   _____
   _____
   _____

Use this space for drawings, pasting pictures, paw prints, or whatever you feel like saving in your journal.

Date: _____

We went to: _____

We saw: _____

We met: _____

I had _____ treats during this adventure!

I pooped _____ time(s) while I was out!

Notes for pawsterity about today:

🐾 _____
_____
_____
_____
_____
_____

Use this space for drawings, pasting pictures, paw prints, or whatever you feel like saving in your journal.

Date: _____

We went to: _____

We saw: _____

We met: _____

I had _____ treats during this adventure!

I pooped _____ time(s) while I was out!

Notes for pawsterity about today:

🐾 _____
_____
_____
_____
_____
_____

Use this space for drawings, pasting pictures, paw prints, or whatever you feel like saving in your journal.

Date: _____

We went to: _____

We saw: _____

We met: _____

I had _____ treats during this adventure!

I pooped _____ time(s) while I was out!

Notes for pawsterity about today:

🐾 _____
_____
_____
_____
_____
_____

Use this space for drawings, pasting pictures, paw prints, or whatever you feel like saving in your journal.

Date: _____

We went to: _____

We saw: _____

We met: _____

I had _____ treats during this adventure!

I pooped _____ time(s) while I was out!

Notes for pawsterity about today:

🐾 _____
_____
_____
_____
_____
_____

Use this space for drawings, pasting pictures, paw prints, or whatever you feel like saving in your journal.

Date: _____

We went to: _____

We saw: _____

We met: _____

I had _____ treats during this adventure!

I pooped _____ time(s) while I was out!

Notes for pawsterity about today:

🐾 _____
_____
_____
_____
_____
_____

Use this space for drawings, pasting pictures, paw prints, or whatever you feel like saving in your journal.

Date: _____

We went to: _____

We saw: _____

We met: _____

I had _____ treats during this adventure!

I pooped _____ time(s) while I was out!

Notes for pawsterity about today:

🐾 _____
_____
_____
_____
_____
_____

Use this space for drawings, pasting pictures, paw prints, or whatever you feel like saving in your journal.

Date: _____

We went to: _____

We saw: _____

We met: _____

I had _____ treats during this adventure!

I pooped _____ time(s) while I was out!

Notes for pawsterity about today:

🐾 _____
_____
_____
_____
_____
_____

Use this space for drawings, pasting pictures, paw prints, or whatever you feel like saving in your journal.

Date: _____

We went to: _____

We saw: _____

We met: _____

I had _____ treats during this adventure!

I pooped _____ time(s) while I was out!

Notes for pawsterity about today:

🐾 _____
_____
_____
_____
_____
_____

Use this space for drawings, pasting pictures, paw prints, or whatever you feel like saving in your journal.

Date: _____

We went to: _____

We saw: _____

We met: _____

I had _____ treats during this adventure!

I pooped _____ time(s) while I was out!

Notes for pawsterity about today:

🐾 _____
_____
_____
_____
_____
_____

Use this space for drawings, pasting pictures, paw prints, or whatever you feel like saving in your journal.

Date: _____

We went to: _____

We saw: _____

We met: _____

I had _____ treats during this adventure!

I pooped _____ time(s) while I was out!

Notes for pawsterity about today:

🐾 _____
_____
_____
_____
_____
_____

Use this space for drawings, pasting pictures, paw prints, or whatever you feel like saving in your journal.

Date: _____

We went to: _____

We saw: _____

We met: _____

I had _____ treats during this adventure!

I pooped _____ time(s) while I was out!

Notes for pawsterity about today:

🐾 _____
_____
_____
_____
_____
_____

Use this space for drawings, pasting pictures, paw prints, or whatever you feel like saving in your journal.

Date: _____

We went to: _____

We saw: _____

We met: _____

I had _____ treats during this adventure!

I pooped _____ time(s) while I was out!

Notes for pawsterity about today:

🐾 _____
_____
_____
_____
_____
_____

Use this space for drawings, pasting pictures, paw prints, or whatever you feel like saving in your journal.

Date: _____

We went to: _____

We saw: _____

We met: _____

I had _____ treats during this adventure!

I pooped _____ time(s) while I was out!

Notes for pawsterity about today:

🐾 _____
_____
_____
_____
_____
_____

Use this space for drawings, pasting pictures, paw prints, or whatever you feel like saving in your journal.

Date: _____

We went to: _____

We saw: _____

We met: _____

I had _____ treats during this adventure!

I pooped _____ time(s) while I was out!

Notes for pawsterity about today:

🐾 _____
_____
_____
_____
_____
_____

Use this space for drawings, pasting pictures, paw prints, or whatever you feel like saving in your journal.

Date: _____

We went to: _____

We saw: _____

We met: _____

I had _____ treats during this adventure!

I pooped _____ time(s) while I was out!

Notes for pawsterity about today:

🐾 _____
_____
_____
_____
_____
_____

Use this space for drawings, pasting pictures, paw prints, or whatever you feel like saving in your journal.

Date: _____

We went to: _____

We saw: _____

We met: _____

I had _____ treats during this adventure!

I pooped _____ time(s) while I was out!

Notes for pawsterity about today:

🐾 _____
_____
_____
_____
_____
_____

Use this space for drawings, pasting pictures, paw prints, or whatever you feel like saving in your journal.

Date: _____

We went to: _____

We saw: _____

We met: _____

I had _____ treats during this adventure!

I pooped _____ time(s) while I was out!

Notes for pawsterity about today:

🐾 _____
_____
_____
_____
_____
_____

Use this space for drawings, pasting pictures, paw prints, or whatever you feel like saving in your journal.

Date: _____

We went to: _____

We saw: _____

We met: _____

I had _____ treats during this adventure!

I pooped _____ time(s) while I was out!

Notes for pawsterity about today:

🐾 _____
_____
_____
_____
_____
_____

Use this space for drawings, pasting pictures, paw prints, or whatever you feel like saving in your journal.

Date: _____

We went to: _____

We saw: _____

We met: _____

I had _____ treats during this adventure!

I pooped _____ time(s) while I was out!

Notes for pawsterity about today:

🐾 _____
_____
_____
_____
_____
_____

Use this space for drawings, pasting pictures, paw prints, or whatever you feel like saving in your journal.

Date: _____

We went to: _____

We saw: _____

We met: _____

I had _____ treats during this adventure!

I pooped _____ time(s) while I was out!

Notes for pawsterity about today:

🐾 _____
_____
_____
_____
_____
_____

Use this space for drawings, pasting pictures, paw prints, or whatever you feel like saving in your journal.

Date: _____

We went to: _____

We saw: _____

We met: _____

I had _____ treats during this adventure!

I pooped _____ time(s) while I was out!

Notes for pawsterity about today:

🐾 _____
_____
_____
_____
_____
_____

Use this space for drawings, pasting pictures, paw prints, or whatever you feel like saving in your journal.

Date: _____

We went to: _____

We saw: _____

We met: _____

I had _____ treats during this adventure!

I pooped _____ time(s) while I was out!

Notes for pawsterity about today:

🐾 _____
_____
_____
_____
_____
_____

Use this space for drawings, pasting pictures, paw prints, or whatever you feel like saving in your journal.

Date: _____

We went to: _____

We saw: _____

We met: _____

I had _____ treats during this adventure!

I pooped _____ time(s) while I was out!

Notes for pawsterity about today:

🐾 _____
_____
_____
_____
_____
_____

Use this space for drawings, pasting pictures, paw prints, or whatever you feel like saving in your journal.

Date: _____

We went to: _____

We saw: _____

We met: _____

I had _____ treats during this adventure!

I pooped _____ time(s) while I was out!

Notes for pawsterity about today:

🐾 _____
_____
_____
_____
_____
_____
_____

Use this space for drawings, pasting pictures, paw prints, or whatever you feel like saving in your journal.

Date: _____

We went to: _____

We saw: _____

We met: _____

I had _____ treats during this adventure!

I pooped _____ time(s) while I was out!

Notes for pawsterity about today:

🐾 _____
_____
_____
_____
_____
_____

Use this space for drawings, pasting pictures, paw prints, or whatever you feel like saving in your journal.

Date: _____

We went to: _____

We saw: _____

We met: _____

I had _____ treats during this adventure!

I pooped _____ time(s) while I was out!

Notes for pawsterity about today:

🐾 _____
_____
_____
_____
_____
_____

Use this space for drawings, pasting pictures, paw prints, or whatever you feel like saving in your journal.

Date: _____
We went to: _____
We saw: _____
We met: _____
I had _____ treats during this adventure!
I pooped _____ time(s) while I was out!
Notes for pawsterity about today:

🐾 _____
_____
_____
_____
_____
_____

Use this space for drawings, pasting pictures, paw prints, or whatever you feel like saving in your journal.

Date: _____

We went to: _____

We saw: _____

We met: _____

I had _____ treats during this adventure!

I pooped _____ time(s) while I was out!

Notes for pawsterity about today:

🐾 _____
_____
_____
_____
_____

Use this space for drawings, pasting pictures, paw prints, or whatever you feel like saving in your journal.

Date: _____

We went to: _____

We saw: _____

We met: _____

I had _____ treats during this adventure!

I pooped _____ time(s) while I was out!

Notes for pawsterity about today:

🐾 _____
_____
_____
_____
_____
_____

Use this space for drawings, pasting pictures, paw prints, or whatever you feel like saving in your journal.

Date: _____

We went to: _____

We saw: _____

We met: _____

I had _____ treats during this adventure!

I pooped _____ time(s) while I was out!

Notes for pawsterity about today:

🐾 _____
_____
_____
_____
_____
_____

Use this space for drawings, pasting pictures, paw prints, or whatever you feel like saving in your journal.

Date: _____

We went to: _____

We saw: _____

We met: _____

I had _____ treats during this adventure!

I pooped _____ time(s) while I was out!

Notes for pawsterity about today:

🐾 _____
_____
_____
_____
_____
_____

Use this space for drawings, pasting pictures, paw prints, or whatever you feel like saving in your journal.

Date: _____

We went to: _____

We saw: _____

We met: _____

I had _____ treats during this adventure!

I pooped _____ time(s) while I was out!

Notes for pawsterity about today:

🐾 _____
_____
_____
_____
_____
_____

Use this space for drawings, pasting pictures, paw prints, or whatever you feel like saving in your journal.

Date: _____

We went to: _____

We saw: _____

We met: _____

I had _____ treats during this adventure!

I pooped _____ time(s) while I was out!

Notes for pawsterity about today:

🐾 _____
_____
_____
_____
_____
_____

Use this space for drawings, pasting pictures, paw prints, or whatever you feel like saving in your journal.

Date: _____

We went to: _____

We saw: _____

We met: _____

I had _____ treats during this adventure!

I pooped _____ time(s) while I was out!

Notes for pawsterity about today:

🐾 _____
_____
_____
_____
_____
_____

Use this space for drawings, pasting pictures, paw prints, or whatever you feel like saving in your journal.

Date: _____

We went to: _____

We saw: _____

We met: _____

I had _____ treats during this adventure!

I pooped _____ time(s) while I was out!

Notes for pawsterity about today:

🐾 _____
_____
_____
_____
_____
_____

Use this space for drawings, pasting pictures, paw prints, or whatever you feel like saving in your journal.

Date: _____

We went to: _____

We saw: _____

We met: _____

I had _____ treats during this adventure!

I pooped _____ time(s) while I was out!

Notes for pawsterity about today:

🐾 _____
     _____
     _____
     _____
     _____
     _____

Use this space for drawings, pasting pictures, paw prints, or whatever you feel like saving in your journal.

Date: _____
We went to: _____
We saw: _____
We met: _____
I had _____ treats during this adventure!
I pooped _____ time(s) while I was out!
Notes for pawsterity about today:

🐾 _____
_____
_____
_____
_____
_____

Use this space for drawings, pasting pictures, paw prints, or whatever you feel like saving in your journal.

Date: _____

We went to: _____

We saw: _____

We met: _____

I had _____ treats during this adventure!

I pooped _____ time(s) while I was out!

Notes for pawsterity about today:

🐾 _____
_____
_____
_____
_____
_____

Use this space for drawings, pasting pictures, paw prints, or whatever you feel like saving in your journal.

Date: _____

We went to: _____

We saw: _____

We met: _____

I had _____ treats during this adventure!

I pooped _____ time(s) while I was out!

Notes for pawsterity about today:

🐾 _____
_____
_____
_____
_____
_____

Use this space for drawings, pasting pictures, paw prints, or whatever you feel like saving in your journal.

Date: _____

We went to: _____

We saw: _____

We met: _____

I had _____ treats during this adventure!

I pooped _____ time(s) while I was out!

Notes for pawsterity about today:

🐾 _____
_____
_____
_____
_____
_____

Use this space for drawings, pasting pictures, paw prints, or whatever you feel like saving in your journal.

Date: _____

We went to: _____

We saw: _____

We met: _____

I had _____ treats during this adventure!

I pooped _____ time(s) while I was out!

Notes for pawsterity about today:

🐾 _____
_____
_____
_____
_____
_____

Use this space for drawings, pasting pictures, paw prints, or whatever you feel like saving in your journal.

Date: _____

We went to: _____

We saw: _____

We met: _____

I had _____ treats during this adventure!

I pooped _____ time(s) while I was out!

Notes for pawsterity about today:

🐾 _____
_____
_____
_____
_____
_____

Use this space for drawings, pasting pictures, paw prints, or whatever you feel like saving in your journal.

Date: _____

We went to: _____

We saw: _____

We met: _____

I had _____ treats during this adventure!

I pooped _____ time(s) while I was out!

Notes for pawsterity about today:

🐾 _____
_____
_____
_____
_____
_____

Use this space for drawings, pasting pictures, paw prints, or whatever you feel like saving in your journal.

Date: _____

We went to: _____

We saw: _____

We met: _____

I had _____ treats during this adventure!

I pooped _____ time(s) while I was out!

Notes for pawsterity about today:

🐾 _____
_____
_____
_____
_____
_____

Use this space for drawings, pasting pictures, paw prints, or whatever you feel like saving in your journal.

Date: _____

We went to: _____

We saw: _____

We met: _____

I had _____ treats during this adventure!

I pooped _____ time(s) while I was out!

Notes for pawsterity about today:

🐾 _____
_____
_____
_____
_____
_____

Use this space for drawings, pasting pictures, paw prints, or whatever you feel like saving in your journal.

Date: _____

We went to: _____

We saw: _____

We met: _____

I had _____ treats during this adventure!

I pooped _____ time(s) while I was out!

Notes for pawsterity about today:

🐾 _____
_____
_____
_____
_____
_____

Use this space for drawings, pasting pictures, paw prints, or whatever you feel like saving in your journal.

Date: _____
We went to: _____
We saw: _____
We met: _____
I had _____ treats during this adventure!
I pooped _____ time(s) while I was out!
Notes for pawsterity about today:

🐾 _____
_____
_____
_____
_____
_____

Use this space for drawings, pasting pictures, paw prints, or whatever you feel like saving in your journal.

Date: _____

We went to: _____

We saw: _____

We met: _____

I had _____ treats during this adventure!

I pooped _____ time(s) while I was out!

Notes for pawsterity about today:

🐾 _____
_____
_____
_____
_____
_____

Use this space for drawings, pasting pictures, paw prints, or whatever you feel like saving in your journal.

Date: _____

We went to: _____

We saw: _____

We met: _____

I had _____ treats during this adventure!

I pooped _____ time(s) while I was out!

Notes for pawsterity about today:

🐾 _____
_____
_____
_____
_____
_____

Use this space for drawings, pasting pictures, paw prints, or whatever you feel like saving in your journal.

Date: _____

We went to: _____

We saw: _____

We met: _____

I had _____ treats during this adventure!

I pooped _____ time(s) while I was out!

Notes for pawsterity about today:

🐾 _____
_____
_____
_____
_____
_____

Use this space for drawings, pasting pictures, paw prints, or whatever you feel like saving in your journal.

Date: _____

We went to: _____

We saw: _____

We met: _____

I had _____ treats during this adventure!

I pooped _____ time(s) while I was out!

Notes for pawsterity about today:

🐾 _____
_____
_____
_____
_____
_____

Use this space for drawings, pasting pictures, paw prints, or whatever you feel like saving in your journal.

Date: _____

We went to: _____

We saw: _____

We met: _____

I had _____ treats during this adventure!

I pooped _____ time(s) while I was out!

Notes for pawsterity about today:

🐾 _____
_____
_____
_____
_____
_____
_____

Use this space for drawings, pasting pictures, paw prints, or whatever you feel like saving in your journal.

Date: _____

We went to: _____

We saw: _____

We met: _____

I had _____ treats during this adventure!

I pooped _____ time(s) while I was out!

Notes for pawsterity about today:

🐾 _____
_____
_____
_____
_____
_____

Use this space for drawings, pasting pictures, paw prints, or whatever you feel like saving in your journal.

Date: _____

We went to: _____

We saw: _____

We met: _____

I had _____ treats during this adventure!

I pooped _____ time(s) while I was out!

Notes for pawsterity about today:

🐾 _____
_____
_____
_____
_____
_____

Use this space for drawings, pasting pictures, paw prints, or whatever you feel like saving in your journal.

Date: _____

We went to: _____

We saw: _____

We met: _____

I had _____ treats during this adventure!

I pooped _____ time(s) while I was out!

Notes for pawsterity about today:

🐾 _____
_____
_____
_____
_____
_____

Use this space for drawings, pasting pictures, paw prints, or whatever you feel like saving in your journal.

Date: _____

We went to: _____

We saw: _____

We met: _____

I had _____ treats during this adventure!

I pooped _____ time(s) while I was out!

Notes for pawsterity about today:

🐾 _____
_____
_____
_____
_____
_____

Use this space for drawings, pasting pictures, paw prints, or whatever you feel like saving in your journal.

Date: _____

We went to: _____

We saw: _____

We met: _____

I had _____ treats during this adventure!

I pooped _____ time(s) while I was out!

Notes for pawsterity about today:

🐾 _____
_____
_____
_____
_____
_____

Use this space for drawings, pasting pictures, paw prints, or whatever you feel like saving in your journal.

Date: _____

We went to: _____

We saw: _____

We met: _____

I had _____ treats during this adventure!

I pooped _____ time(s) while I was out!

Notes for pawsterity about today:

🐾 _____
_____
_____
_____
_____
_____

Use this space for drawings, pasting pictures, paw prints, or whatever you feel like saving in your journal.

Date: _____

We went to: _____

We saw: _____

We met: _____

I had _____ treats during this adventure!

I pooped _____ time(s) while I was out!

Notes for pawsterity about today:

🐾 _____
_____
_____
_____
_____
_____

Use this space for drawings, pasting pictures, paw prints, or whatever you feel like saving in your journal.

Date: _____

We went to: _____

We saw: _____

We met: _____

I had _____ treats during this adventure!

I pooped _____ time(s) while I was out!

Notes for pawsterity about today:

🐾 _____
_____
_____
_____
_____
_____

Use this space for drawings, pasting pictures, paw prints, or whatever you feel like saving in your journal.

Date: _____

We went to: _____

We saw: _____

We met: _____

I had _____ treats during this adventure!

I pooped _____ time(s) while I was out!

Notes for pawsterity about today:

🐾 _____
_____
_____
_____
_____
_____

Use this space for drawings, pasting pictures, paw prints, or whatever you feel like saving in your journal.

Date: _____

We went to: _____

We saw: _____

We met: _____

I had _____ treats during this adventure!

I pooped _____ time(s) while I was out!

Notes for pawsterity about today:

🐾 _____
_____
_____
_____
_____
_____

Use this space for drawings, pasting pictures, paw prints, or whatever you feel like saving in your journal.

Date: _____

We went to: _____

We saw: _____

We met: _____

I had _____ treats during this adventure!

I pooped _____ time(s) while I was out!

Notes for pawsterity about today:

🐾 _____
_____
_____
_____
_____
_____

Use this space for drawings, pasting pictures, paw prints, or whatever you feel like saving in your journal.

Date: _____

We went to: _____

We saw: _____

We met: _____

I had _____ treats during this adventure!

I pooped _____ time(s) while I was out!

Notes for pawsterity about today:

🐾 _____
_____
_____
_____
_____
_____

Use this space for drawings, pasting pictures, paw prints, or whatever you feel like saving in your journal.

Date: _____

We went to: _____

We saw: _____

We met: _____

I had _____ treats during this adventure!

I pooped _____ time(s) while I was out!

Notes for pawsterity about today:

🐾 _____
_____
_____
_____
_____
_____

Use this space for drawings, pasting pictures, paw prints, or whatever you feel like saving in your journal.

Date: _____

We went to: _____

We saw: _____

We met: _____

I had _____ treats during this adventure!

I pooped _____ time(s) while I was out!

Notes for pawsterity about today:

🐾 _____
_____
_____
_____
_____
_____

Use this space for drawings, pasting pictures, paw prints, or whatever you feel like saving in your journal.

Date: _____

We went to: _____

We saw: _____

We met: _____

I had _____ treats during this adventure!

I pooped _____ time(s) while I was out!

Notes for pawsterity about today:

🐾 _____
_____
_____
_____
_____
_____

Use this space for drawings, pasting pictures, paw prints, or whatever you feel like saving in your journal.

Date: _____

We went to: _____

We saw: _____

We met: _____

I had _____ treats during this adventure!

I pooped _____ time(s) while I was out!

Notes for pawsterity about today:

🐾 _____
_____
_____
_____
_____
_____

Use this space for drawings, pasting pictures, paw prints, or whatever you feel like saving in your journal.

Use these pages to paste even more pictures and stories of your adventures!

It's been a ton of fun to be part of your adventures! Share pics of your pages on social media and make sure you tag me so I can see how much fun you are having!

For more journals, books, and fun, check out my author page on Amazon!

amazon.com/author/pamrobertson

You'll also find some interesting stuff here on the website
www.ladybirdfiles.com

by
Pam Robertson
Call 780-232-0083
Facebook BeBoldBeBraveBeBrilliant
Twitter @PamRobertson
IG @PamDRobertson
www.ladybirdfiles.com

Made in the USA
Charleston, SC
30 October 2016